COOKING WITH GRAINS

coleen & bob simmons

TAYLOR TRADE PUBLISHING

Cooking with Grains, Revised Edition, a nitty gritty® Cookbook

©2013 by Taylor Trade Publishing
An imprint of
The Rowman & Littlefield Publishing Group, Inc.
4501 Forbes Boulevard, Suite 200
Lanham, MD 20706
www.rowman.com

Produced by CulinartMedia, Inc.
Design: Harrah Lord
Layout: Patty Holden
Photography: Eising Food Photography (all rights reserved)
www.culinartmedia.com

Distributed by National Book Network
1-800-462-6420

ISBN 978-1-58979-888-5
Library of Congress Cataloguing-in-Publication Data on file

Printed in China

CONTENTS

THE BASICS

In 1990, the USDA revamped its dietary guidelines. The new system is represented graphically by a "food guide pyramid." As its foundation, the guidelines recommend grain products, such as bread, cereal, rice, and pasta, and suggest daily servings of fruits and vegetables to round out meals. Meat, dairy products, fats, and oils should be served sparingly.

This book attempts to provide interesting recipes to help you incorporate more grains into your diet. This is not a vegetarian cookbook, but many of the recipes are meatless. Our main goals were to use grains in recipes that taste good and to utilize some of the less familiar grains.

TIPS FOR COOKING WITH GRAINS

• Purchase grains from a high-volume source, particularly if you buy them in bulk. Seek out the best health food store or ethnic market in your area. Or, purchase grains through a reputable mail-order source.

• Buy only the amount of grains you need or think you will use within 2 to 3 weeks. Whole grains, which still have the germ intact, turn rancid quickly.

• Store grains and grain flours in a cool dark place, preferably in glass jars or plastic containers with tight-fitting lids. In warm, humid climates, store grains in the refrigerator or freezer. Check grains and flours periodically for insects and immediately discard any with signs of infestation.

• Grains have varying moisture contents. Testing and tasting them while cooking is the best way to assure that grains are properly cooked. Older, drier grains usually take longer to cook than do younger, moister ones. All cooking times in this book are approximate.

• An electric crockery pot is a very useful tool for cooking whole grains, particularly those that require long soaking and cooking times. Most grain berries cook from start to finish in 3 to 4 hours in a crockery pot without soaking. Experiment with your model to determine cooking times.

• Cook grains in quantity when you have time and refrigerate them for up to 2 days or freeze them in airtight containers. It is easy to put together recipes when you already have cooked grains on hand.

BASIC STOCKS

BASIC BEEF STOCK

MAKES ABOUT 6 CUPS

Homemade beef stock adds a terrific flavor to soups and sauces and it is well worth the time and effort needed to make your own. It is easy to make homemade stocks: just brown the bones and vegetables in the oven, put them in a pot with water and let the stock simmer on the back of the stove for several hours while you are doing something else. You can make the stock ahead of time and freeze it in convenient portions for later use.

5 lb. beef soup bones, preferably with
    a small amount of meat attached
3 medium onions, quartered
4 carrots, cut into 1-inch pieces

2 stalks celery with leaves, cut into 1-inch pieces
8 black peppercorns
3 Tbsp. tomato paste

Heat oven to 450°F. Wipe bones with a damp paper towel and place in a low-sided roasting pan or sturdy rimmed baking sheet. Brown bones in oven for 45 minutes, turning once. Add onions and carrots to pan and continue to roast for 15 to 20 minutes, until vegetables are browned; check to see that vegetables do not burn. Place browned meat, onions, and carrots in a large stockpot with celery, peppercorns, and enough cold water to cover meat and vegetables. Pour off fat from roasting pan and discard. Add about 1 cup water to roasting pan and scrape up the browned bits from pan with a spatula. Add to stockpot. Bring stock to a boil over high heat, skimming and discarding any foam that rises to the top. Reduce heat to low and simmer slowly for at least 4 hours.

Strain stock through a fine sieve into a clean pot. Discard solids. Cool stock rapidly by placing pot in a sink filled with ice water and stirring frequently until cooled to at least room temperature. Cover stock and refrigerate overnight.

Remove and discard any congealed fat on the surface of chilled stock. Bring stock to a boil over high heat. Stir in tomato paste, reduce heat to low and simmer until stock is reduced to about 6 cups. Cool and refrigerate for 3 to 4 days or freeze until ready to use.

Stock can be reduced even further if you want a very rich, concentrated broth, or if freezer space is at a premium. Add a little water to bring up the volume when using for soup or other recipes.

BASIC CHICKEN STOCK

MAKES ABOUT 10 CUPS

4–5 lb. chicken parts, carcasses, bones, hearts, and/or gizzards
1 large onion, unpeeled
2 large carrots, unpeeled, cut into 1-inch pieces
2 large stalks celery with leaves, cut into 1-inch pieces
2 large sprigs fresh parsley with stems
6–8 black peppercorns
1 bay leaf

When chickens are on sale, buy 3 or 4. Cut them up and freeze the breasts for a quick stir-fry or sautéed chicken entrée. Marinate the legs in your favorite teriyaki sauce and bake them for a picnic or lunchbox. Reserve the wing tips for the stock and marinate the wings in a zesty barbecue sauce before grilling. The rest of the chicken, except for the liver, goes into the stockpot. Each time you cook a chicken, save and freeze the uncooked necks and trimmings. Soon there will be enough chicken parts to make a delicious pot of stock. The frozen parts don't have to be thawed before putting them in the stockpot. Onion and carrot peels give the stock a rich color and flavor.

Place chicken parts in a large stockpot with enough cold water to cover chicken by at least 2 inches. Bring stock to a boil over high heat, skimming and discarding any foam that rises to the top. Add remaining ingredients and bring back to a boil. Reduce heat to low and simmer slowly for 3 to 4 hours.

Strain stock through a fine sieve into a clean pot. Discard solids. Cool stock rapidly by placing pot in a sink filled with ice water and stirring frequently until cooled. When stock is at room temperature, cover and refrigerate overnight.

Remove and discard any congealed fat on the surface of chilled stock. Bring stock to a boil over high heat, reduce heat to low and simmer until stock is reduced to about 10 cups. Cool and refrigerate for 3 to 4 days or freeze until ready to use.

Stock can be reduced even further if you want a very rich, concentrated broth, or if freezer space is at a premium. Add a little water to bring up the volume when using for soup or other recipes.

BASIC VEGETABLE STOCK

MAKES 5 TO 6 CUPS

This stock is a perfect foundation for risottos, bean dishes, or soups. You can vary the vegetables to suit the dish you are preparing. For example, if you are making a springtime risotto with asparagus and peas, add 5 to 6 asparagus spears to the stock to reinforce the asparagus flavor of the finished dish.

1 medium onion, peeled
2–3 large carrots, scrubbed
2 stalks celery with leaves
1 large leek, well washed
1 medium russet potato, scrubbed
4–5 cloves garlic, smashed
1 jalapeño chile, stemmed and seeded, or ¼ tsp. red pepper flakes

1 Tbsp. vegetable or olive oil
6–8 whole fresh parsley stems
5–6 sprigs fresh thyme
2 bay leaves
4–5 black peppercorns
1 tsp. salt
½ cup dry vermouth or white wine, optional
2 qt. water

Coarsely chop onion, carrots, celery, leek, potato, garlic, and jalapeño. In a large heavy stockpot heat oil over medium-high heat and sauté chopped vegetables for 5 to 10 minutes, until lightly browned and fragrant. Add remaining ingredients and bring stock to a boil over high heat. Reduce heat to low and simmer uncovered for 45 to 60 minutes. Strain stock and discard solids. Cool. Cover and refrigerate for 3 to 4 days or freeze until ready to use.

WHEAT & BARLEY

ABOUT WHEAT

Since the cultivation and consumption of wheat predates written history, it is difficult to determine when it was first eaten. Wheat slowly replaced other local grains as it traveled. As a result more hardy wheat strains with higher yields were developed over time. Today, almost all diets are based on either wheat or rice.

Wheat is high in fiber and vitamins B and E and it provides some protein. Much of the wheat consumed in this country is in the form of bread or pastry, which are made from highly processed "white" wheat flour. Unfortunately, many of the nutrients in wheat are removed by the milling process.

Wheat berries are whole wheat kernels from which the hull has been removed. Wheat berries have a some-what meaty texture and are good sub-stitutes for ground meat in recipes. Hard wheat berries come from high-protein "hard" wheat strains. Soft wheat berries come from low-protein "soft" wheat strains. Hard wheat berries take a little longer to cook than soft wheat berries, but they are interchangeable in recipes.

Cracked wheat is produced by cut-ting the wheat berry into 2 or 3 pieces. It can be added to breads or used as a substitute for wheat berries or bulgur.

Bulgur is wheat that has been precooked by either steaming or par-boiling, after which it is dried, cracked and separated into grades of fine, medium and coarse. Bulgur is easy to cook and its tender, chewy texture makes it perfect for salads, pilafs, savory stuffing and hearty soups. It is also makes a lovely breakfast cereal.

Spelt is an ancient form of wheat that has a high protein content. Spelt berries are interchangeable with wheat berries.

Couscous is a type of tiny pasta that is made from wheat flour. Traditional couscous is made from cracked semo-lina, a strain of hard wheat. Couscous is a versatile grain and cooks quickly. In North Africa couscous is used as the base for a dish of the same name, in which the couscous is steamed in a "couscousiere" over an aromatic meat and vegetable stew. The quick-cooking couscous found in markets generally steams in 5 minutes in boiling liquid and is excellent as a side dish or in a salad.

Israeli couscous is a wheat product with "kernels" about the size of pep-percorns. It can be cooked like risotto or boiled like pasta and served topped with a sauce or tossed into a salad. Look for Israeli couscous in a Middle Eastern market or specialty food store.

ABOUT BARLEY

Like wheat, barley consumption predates written history. Nomadic tribes began cultivating barley first as a cereal grain and soon after as a beer-brewing ingredient. Barley is full of vitamins and is a good source of fiber, complex carbohydrates and protein. Barley is low in fat and has no cholesterol.

While barley has a more distinctive flavor than rice, it, like rice, is a delicious base for soups, stews, salads, curries, casseroles and desserts.

Pearl barley is whole-grain barley from which the outer hull has been removed. It is the most common form available. Pearl barley comes in both regular and quick-cooking forms.

Barley flakes make a delicious hot cereal. Cook them as you would oatmeal or use in baked goods.

Barley flour is a low-gluten flour. It can be used in baked items to add a distinc-tive flavor, but it should be combined with wheat flour to achieve the proper results. In general, you can replace up to 25% of the wheat flour with barley flour in yeast breads and up to 50% of the wheat flour with barley flour in cookies and quick breads.

BASIC SOAKED BULGUR OR CRACKED WHEAT

MAKES 2 CUPS

Bulgur and cracked wheat have a toasty, nutty flavor. Soaked bulgur or cracked wheat are usually used for cold dishes like Tabbouleh Salad, page 16.

1 cup fine-, medium-, or coarse-grained bulgur, or cracked wheat
Cold water or stock if using fine-grained bulgur, boiling water or stock if using medium-or coarse-grained bulgur, or cracked wheat

Place bulgur in a bowl and cover with cold or boiling water. Let stand for 30 minutes; drain. Fluff grains with a fork. Makes 2 cups

BASIC COOKED BULGUR OR CRACKED WHEAT

MAKES 2 CUPS

Cooked bulgur or cracked wheat are usually used for hot dishes or when you need it quickly. Cooking bulgur or cracked wheat takes about half as long as soaking it, but it will take extra time to cool if you are using it in a cold dish.

About 2 cups water, stock, or other
  flavored liquid
1 cup fine-, medium-, or coarse-grained
  bulgur, or cracked wheat

Place water in a saucepan and bring to a boil. Add bulgur, reduce heat to low and simmer for 15 to 20 minutes; drain. Fluff grains with a fork.

BASIC COOKED WHEAT BERRIES

MAKES 2½ TO 3 CUPS

Like dried beans, wheat berries must be soaked before they are cooked. The texture of cooked wheat berries is similar to fresh corn. Do not add salt during cooking or it could toughen the berries or lengthen the cooking time.

1 cup hard or soft wheat berries
3½ cups cold water, plus water to cover

Place wheat berries in a large bowl and cover with water. Let stand covered overnight; drain. *Quick Soak Method*: Place wheat berries in a saucepan, cover with water and bring to a boil. Remove from heat and let stand for 1 hour; drain. In a saucepan, bring 3½ cups water to a boil over high heat. Add soaked wheat berries. Reduce heat to low, cover and simmer for 55 to 60 minutes, until tender.

BASIC COOKED SPELT BERRIES

MAKES 2 CUPS

Spelt has a delicious, nutty flavor and more protein and B vitamins than wheat.

1 cup spelt berries
3 cups cold water, plus water to cover

Place spelt berries in a large bowl and cover with cold water. Let stand covered for at least 6 hours or overnight. *Quick Soak Method*: Place spelt berries in a saucepan, cover with water and bring to a boil. Remove from heat and let stand for 1 hour; drain.

In a saucepan, bring 3 cups water to a boil over high heat. Add soaked spelt berries. Reduce heat to low, cover and simmer for about 45 minutes, until tender.

QUICK-COOKING COUSCOUS

MAKES ABOUT 3 CUPS

Look for couscous that's labeled "instant."

1½ cups boiling water or stock
1–2 Tbsp. butter
1 cup quick-cooking couscous

Combine ingredients in a saucepan, cover pan and let stand for 5 minutes. Remove lid and fluff grains with a fork.

BASIC COOKED ISRAELI COUSCOUS

MAKES ABOUT 2 CUPS

Israeli couscous must be tasted during cooking to judge whether or not it is done. You can vary this recipe by adding spices and herbs to the liquid.

1 Tbsp. olive oil or butter
½ cup finely diced onion, optional
1 cup Israeli couscous
1½ cups boiling water or stock
¼ tsp. salt

In a medium skillet, heat oil over medium heat. Add onion, sauté for 5 to 6 minutes until softened. Add couscous and stir for 1 to 2 minutes, until grains are coated with oil. Add water and salt. Cover pan, reduce heat to low and simmer for 8 to 10 minutes, stirring occasionally. Remove from heat; let stand covered for 5 minutes. Fluff grains with a fork.

BASIC COOKED PEARL BARLEY

MAKES 3½ TO 4 CUPS

Pearl barley requires no soaking. Take a couple of minutes to sort through it and remove any stones or extraneous materials. Instant or quick-cooking barley usually cooks in 10 to 12 minutes. Follow package directions for specifics.

1 cup regular pearl barley
3 cups water or stock
½ tsp. salt, if using water

Place barley, water and salt, if using, in a medium saucepan and bring to a boil over high heat. Reduce heat to low, cover, and cook for about 45 minutes, until barley is tender and most of the liquid is absorbed. Fluff grains with a fork. Cool before refrigerating.

SPICED BREAKFAST BULGUR

SERVES 4

Hot bulgur with dried fruit and spices makes a great breakfast cereal.

1 cup medium-grained bulgur
2½ cups milk, plus more for serving
Pinch salt
3 Tbsp. honey, plus more for serving, optional

½ cup raisins, dried cranberries, or dried
   apple pieces
½ tsp. cinnamon sugar for serving, optional

In a large saucepan, combine bulgur, milk, salt, honey, raisins, and cinnamon and bring to a boil. Reduce heat to low and simmer for 20 minutes, until mixture thickens, stirring frequently. Pour into serving bowls and pass milk and honey or sugar.

SPELT BERRY, WALNUT & CORN SALAD

SERVES 4 TO 6

Walnut oil lends a distinct nutty flavor to this salad. Buy walnut oil in small bottles and refrigerate it after opening to avoid spoiling. Cooked wheat berries or barley are also good in this salad.

2½ cups Basic Cooked Spelt Berries, page 12
½ cup cooked corn kernels
½ cup diced roasted red bell pepper
½ cup chopped toasted walnuts
1 jalapeño chile, stemmed, seeded, and
    finely minced

5 green onions, white part only, minced
2 Tbsp. chopped fresh parsley
Salt and freshly ground pepper, to taste
3 Tbsp. walnut oil
1 Tbsp. sherry vinegar

In a large bowl, combine spelt berries, corn, red pepper, walnuts, jalapeño, onions, and parsley and mix well. Season with salt and pepper. In a small bowl, whisk walnut oil and sherry wine vinegar together; pour over salad and toss well. Check seasonings and serve.

TABBOULEH SALAD

SERVES 6

Serve this lemony Middle Eastern bulgur and herb salad with lettuce or Belgian endive leaves for scooping. It is a nice accompaniment to grilled meats. To save time, wash and dry parsley in a salad spinner and chop it with a food processor. For a delicious variation, stir 1 cup chopped, peeled, and seeded tomatoes and ½ cup diced cucumber into the finished salad.

Basic Soaked Bulgur, page 11, medium-grain
1½ cups chopped fresh parsley
¼ cup chopped fresh mint
5–6 green onions, minced
1 clove garlic, minced
Grated peel (zest) from 2 lemons

⅓ – ½ cup lemon juice
¼ cup full-flavored olive oil
Salt and freshly ground pepper, to taste
⅓ cup pine nuts, toasted, or chopped
   toasted walnuts

Drain bulgur and squeeze very dry with your hands, discarding soaking liquid. Place bulgur in a serving bowl with parsley, mint, green onions, garlic, and lemon zest. In a small bowl, whisk lemon juice, olive oil, salt, and pepper until mixed. Pour lemon juice mixture over bulgur mixture and toss lightly. Cover and refrigerate for 1 to 2 hours, or serve immediately. Stir in pine nuts just before serving.

ASPARAGUS COUSCOUS SALAD

SERVES 4 TO 6

This salad, perfect as a side dish for grilled fish or chicken, can be made ahead of time, refrigerated, and brought back to room temperature before serving.

6 cups water
2 tsp. salt
¾ lb. thin asparagus spears, trimmed
2 Tbsp. butter
1½ cups quick-cooking couscous
2 Tbsp. rice vinegar

1 Tbsp. sugar
1 tsp. finely grated fresh ginger
2 Tbsp. toasted sesame oil
Salt and freshly ground pepper, to taste
½ cup diced roasted red bell pepper
½ cup thinly sliced green onions

In a large saucepan, bring 4 cups of the water to a boil. Add 1 teaspoon of the salt and asparagus spears and cook for 4 to 5 minutes until crisp-tender. Drain and plunge into a bowl of ice water for 5 minutes; drain and pat dry with paper towels. In a saucepan, bring butter, remaining 2 cups water, and 1 teaspoon salt to a boil. Add couscous, bring back to a boil and cook for 2 minutes. Cover, remove from heat and let stand for 5 minutes. Fluff grains with a fork and cool for a few minutes. In a small bowl, combine vinegar, sugar, and ginger; whisk in sesame oil and season with salt and pepper. Pour couscous into a bowl with red pepper, green onions, and dressing and toss gently. Top with asparagus spears.

CORN & BULGUR FRITTATA

SERVES 4

This colorful frittata makes a great brunch dish or lunchbox treat. Use fine grained bulgur for this dish. Soak the bulgur while preparing the rest of the recipe ingredients. Other cooked grain berries, such as pearl barley or spelt, can be substituted for bulgur.

About 1 cup Basic Soaked Bulgur or Cracked Wheat, page 11
1 Tbsp. plus 2 tsp. olive oil
½ cup finely chopped onion
Kernels from 1 ear fresh corn, about ½ cup
1 small zucchini, trimmed, cut in half lengthwise and thinly sliced
1 small tomato, peeled, seeded, and chopped
Salt and freshly ground pepper to taste
7 large eggs
3–4 drops Tabasco Sauce
2 Tbsp. chopped fresh parsley
2 Tbsp. freshly grated Parmesan cheese

Drain bulgur, squeeze dry, and set aside. In a large skillet, heat 1 tablespoon of the olive oil over medium heat and sauté onion for 6 to 8 minutes, until softened. Add corn, zucchini, tomato, soaked bulgur, salt, and pepper and mix well. Cook for 2 to 3 minutes. Remove from heat.

Heat oven to 450°F. In a large bowl, beat eggs, salt, pepper, Tabasco, and parsley with a fork until well mixed. Add sautéed vegetables and mix well. Heat remaining 2 teaspoons oil in an ovenproof 10-inch nonstick skillet. Pour egg mixture into heated skillet and cook until eggs start to set. Tilt pan and, with a fork, pull eggs from around sides of pan so uncooked portion flows under cooked portion. When top of eggs is no longer liquid, sprinkle with Parmesan cheese and place in oven for 5 to 8 minutes, until top is firm and lightly browned.

Remove skillet from oven, invert a plate on top of skillet and flip frittata onto plate. Invert a serving plate on top of frittata and flip again onto serving plate. Blot any excess oil from surface with paper towels. Cut into wedges and serve warm or at room temperature.

PASTA WITH TOMATO-WHEAT BERRY SAUCE

SERVES 4

Wheat berries add a meaty texture to this zesty tomato sauce. Start cooking the pasta when the sauce has about 10 minutes left to cook so that the pasta and the sauce will be ready at the same time.

2 Tbsp. full-flavored olive oil
1 small onion, finely chopped
¼ tsp. red pepper flakes
⅓ cup finely chopped red bell pepper
⅓ cup finely chopped celery
3 cloves garlic, minced
¼ cup finely diced ham, or 2 to 3 thin slices prosciutto, finely chopped
2 cans (14 oz. each) ready-cut tomatoes
⅓ cup dry red wine
½ tsp. ground anise
1½ tsp. dried oregano
1½ cups Basic Cooked Wheat Berries, page 12
Salt and freshly ground pepper, to taste
1 Tbsp. salt
12 oz. fusilli, orecchiette, or other dried pasta shapes
2 Tbsp. chopped fresh parsley
Freshly grated Parmesan cheese

In a large skillet, heat olive oil over medium heat and sauté onion, pepper flakes, red pepper, and celery for 5 to 6 minutes. Add garlic and ham and cook for 1 minute. Add tomatoes, wine, anise, oregano, wheat berries, salt, and pepper. Reduce heat to low and simmer sauce uncovered for 30 minutes, stirring occasionally.

In a large pot, bring 5 to 6 quarts water to a boil over high heat. Add salt and cook pasta according to package directions, draining it about 1 minute before it is completely cooked. Pour drained pasta into cooked sauce and continue to cook for about 1 minute, until pasta is done. Pour pasta and sauce into heated serving bowls and sprinkle with parsley and Parmesan cheese. Serve immediately.

RHUBARB CRISP

SERVES 6

This old-fashioned crisp is still a current-day crowd-pleaser. Organic wheat flakes, not whole wheat breakfast cereal, are used in the crunchy brown sugar topping. If you like, pass a little heavy cream to pour over the top or serve with vanilla ice cream.

1½ lb. rhubarb, trimmed and cut into
   ½-inch pieces
1¼ cups brown sugar, packed
⅓ cup all-purpose flour
1 tsp. cinnamon

2 Tbsp. Triple Sec or other orange liqueur
5 Tbsp. butter
¼ cup all-purpose flour
Pinch salt
1 cup wheat flakes, rolled oats or kamut flakes

Heat oven to 375°F. Lightly oil an 8 x 8 x 2-inch baking pan. In a large bowl, toss rhubarb with ¾ cup of the brown sugar, ⅓ cup flour, cinnamon, and Triple Sec. In a food processor, combine butter, ¼ cup flour, remaining ½ cup brown sugar, and salt. Pulse several times until butter mixture is the size of small peas. Transfer mixture to a medium bowl and combine with wheat flakes. Pour rhubarb mixture into baking pan and spread evenly. Distribute topping evenly over rhubarb. Bake for 35 to 40 minutes, until topping is lightly browned and rhubarb mixture is bubbling. Serve warm or at room temperature.

SPELT BERRY SLOPPY JOES
SERVES 4 TO 6

These sure kid-pleasers go together quickly if you have cooked spelt or wheat berries in the refrigerator. You won't even miss the meat!

1 Tbsp. vegetable oil
1 small onion, finely chopped
1 can (8 oz.) tomato sauce
2 Tbsp. tomato paste
2 tsp. chili powder
1 tsp. dry mustard
1 Tbsp. brown sugar
2 tsp. apple cider vinegar

½ tsp. celery salt
2 tsp. Worcestershire sauce
½ tsp. Tabasco Jalapeño Sauce, optional
Freshly ground black pepper, to taste
2 cups Basic Cooked Spelt Berries or Basic Cooked
    Wheat Berries, page 12
4–6 small soft hamburger buns, lightly toasted

In a medium skillet heat oil over low heat. Add onion and cook for 6 to 8 minutes, until soft and lightly browned. Stir in tomato sauce, tomato paste, chili powder, mustard, sugar, vinegar, celery salt, Worcestershire, Tabasco, and pepper. Cook over medium heat until bubbling. Add spelt berries, heat through and check seasonings. Serve on hamburger buns.

CURRIED CARROT BARLEY SOUP

SERVES 4

This soup can be made in less than an hour if you use quick-cooking barley. Slice the onions and carrots with a food processor for ease.

3 Tbsp. butter
1 small onion, thinly sliced
Pinch red pepper flakes
2 tsp. curry powder
½ cup quick-cooking barley
1 Tbsp. brown sugar
1 lb. carrots, peeled and thinly sliced

4 cups Basic Chicken Stock, page 7,
    or canned chicken broth
1 Tbsp. lemon juice
Salt and freshly ground pepper
Plain yogurt for garnish
Fresh cilantro leaves for garnish

In a heavy saucepan, melt butter over medium heat and sauté onion for 5 to 6 minutes, until soft. Add pepper flakes and curry and cook for 1 minute. Add barley and brown sugar and cook for 2 to 3 minutes, stirring to coat barley with butter-curry mixture. Add carrots and chicken stock and bring to a boil. Reduce heat to low and simmer covered for 30 minutes, until vegetables are tender. Remove from heat and cool for a few minutes. In batches, carefully purée soup with a blender or food processor and return to pan. Stir in lemon juice, salt, and pepper. Serve hot, garnished with yogurt and cilantro. If desired, this soup can be cooled and refrigerated for a few days or frozen until needed.

MUSHROOM BARLEY SOUP

SERVES 4 TO 6

Serve this soup, which freezes well, for a rainy-day meal with hot garlic bread or biscuits. Soaked wheat berries, page 12, can be substituted for barley.

1 oz. dried porcini or shiitake mushrooms
6 cups hot water
2 Tbsp. butter
2 Tbsp. olive oil
2 large onions, chopped
4 medium carrots, peeled and chopped
1 lb. fresh cremini (brown) mushrooms,
   coarsely chopped

⅔ cup regular pearl barley
4 sprigs fresh parsley
2 sprigs fresh thyme
1 bay leaf
6 cups Basic Beef Stock, page 6,
   or canned beef broth
¾ tsp. salt
Generous grinds black pepper

Place dried mushrooms in a small bowl with 2 cups of the hot water; let stand for 20 minutes, until softened. Remove mushrooms from liquid and chop coarsley. Strain soaking liquid through a paper coffee filter or cheesecloth and reserve.

In a medium stockpot, heat butter and olive oil over low heat. Add onions and carrots and sauté for 5 to 7 minutes. Increase heat to medium-high, add fresh mushrooms and sauté for 3 minutes. Add barley and cook for 2 minutes. Add parsley, thyme, bay leaf, stock, mushroom liquid, and remaining 4 cups hot water. Simmer uncovered for 45 minutes, until barley is soft. Adjust seasonings and serve.

MIDDLE EASTERN BARLEY SALAD

SERVES 4 TO 6

This soup can be made in less than an hour if you use quick-cooking barley. Slice the onions and carrots with a food processor for ease.

2 cups Basic Cooked Pearl Barley, page 13, room temperature
4–5 green onions, white part only, thinly sliced
1 medium-sized red bell pepper, stemmed, seeded and diced
1 large stalk celery, cut into ¼-inch dice
1 cup diced seeded cucumber
1 cup diced peeled, seeded tomato
⅓ cup chopped kalamata olives
¼ cup capers, rinsed and drained

⅓ cup chopped fresh mint
¼ cup chopped fresh parsley
¼ cup full-flavored olive oil
2 tbs. lemon juice
1 clove garlic, finely minced
½ tsp. dried oregano
½ tsp. ground cumin
Salt and freshly ground pepper to taste
½ cup crumbled feta cheese, optional
Pita pockets or lettuce leaves for serving

In a large bowl, combine cooked barley, onions, red pepper, celery, cucumber, tomato, olives, capers, mint, and parsley and toss well. In a small bowl, whisk together olive oil, lemon juice, garlic, oregano, cumin, salt, and pepper. Pour dressing over barley mixture and toss well. If desired, sprinkle with crumbled feta cheese. Serve in pita pockets or lettuce leaves. Salad can be made ahead and refrigerated for a few hours; remove from refrigerator at least 30 minutes before serving.

CHOCOLATE BARLEY NUGGETS

MAKES 80

Tuck these into a lunchbox or serve them with an afternoon cup of tea. For easy cleanup, line baking sheets with parchment paper. You can replace ¾ cup of the all-purpose flour with barley or oat flour, if desired.

2 squares (1 oz. each) unsweetened
   baking chocolate
¾ cup vegetable shortening
1 cup granulated sugar
¼ cup brown sugar, packed
1 large egg
1 tsp. vanilla extract
2 Tbsp. dark rum or brandy, optional

1½ cups all-purpose flour
1 tsp. baking soda
½ tsp. salt
1 tsp. cinnamon
½ cup buttermilk
1½ cups barley flakes
½ cup chopped pecans

Heat oven to 350°F. Melt chocolate in a small bowl over a pan of hot water, or microwave on HIGH for 60 to 90 seconds, stirring after 30 seconds. Cool slightly. With a mixer, beat shortening with sugars until light and fluffy. Add egg, vanilla, rum, if using, and melted chocolate and mix well. In a small bowl, stir together flour, soda, salt, and cinnamon. Mix flour mixture into chocolate mixture alternately with buttermilk. Stir in barley flakes and pecans. Drop rounded teaspoonfuls of dough onto baking sheets. Bake for about 15 minutes, or until cookies are firm to the touch. Cool on a rack.

CURRANT SCONES

SERVES 4

These are perfect for a special breakfast or a winter afternoon tea. Oat or millet flour can be substituted for barley flour. Serve with butter and fruit preserves.

1½ cups all-purpose flour
½ cup barley flour
⅓ cup sugar
2 tsp. baking powder
¼ tsp. salt

½ cup butter, cut into pieces
1 large egg, lightly beaten
⅔–¾ cup milk
⅓ cup currants

Heat oven to 400°F. In a large bowl, stir together flours, sugar, baking powder, and salt. With a pastry blender or 2 forks, cut in butter until butter mixture is the size of small peas. Add egg and mix well. Gradually add milk and mix until dough is sticky, but workable. Stir in raisins.

On a piece of parchment paper or well-floured work surface, spoon dough into a circle about 1 inch thick. Transfer dough and parchment, if using, to an ungreased baking sheet. With a knife, score dough into 8 wedges. Bake for 25 to 30 minutes, until puffed and golden brown. Cut into wedges and serve hot.

PLUM CAKE

SERVES 8

Barley flour is used in this moist, homestyle fruit-topped cake. A scoop of rich vanilla ice cream is a delicious accent.

½ cup butter
1 cup plus 2 Tbsp. sugar
2 large eggs
1 tsp. vanilla extract
Grated peel (zest) from 1 lemon
½ cup barley flour

½ cup all-purpose flour
1 tsp. baking powder
⅛ tsp. salt
6 medium-sized fresh plums,
    pitted and cut into quarters
½ tsp. cinnamon

Heat oven to 350°F. Butter a 9-inch springform pan. With a mixer, beat ½ cup butter with 1 cup sugar until light and fluffy, about 2 minutes. Add eggs, vanilla, and lemon zest and mix well. In a small bowl, combine flours, baking powder and salt, and whisk to combine. Add flour mixture to egg mixture and beat on high speed for 2 minutes, until batter is stiff and smooth. Spread batter in prepared pan. Arrange plums on top of batter and sprinkle with 2 tablespoons sugar and cinnamon. Bake cake for 45 minutes, until cake pulls away from the sides of pan and a toothpick inserted into the center comes out clean. Cool on a rack for 10 minutes. Run a thin knife around the edge of cake and release it from pan. Cool on a rack. Cut into wedges and serve at room temperature.

RICE & WILD RICE

ABOUT RICE

Rice as we know it was most likely developed when wild grasses were domesticated about 5,000 years ago. Rice thrives in warm climates where there is a good water supply. Thousands of varieties of rice are grown around the world. Several imported varieties are now widely available in the United States, including basmati from India, jasmine from Thailand, and Arborio from Italy.

Rice is a very important ingredient in the diet of over half the world's population. In many cultures it is consumed 3 times a day. Rice has a fair amount of protein B vitamins, phosphorus and magnesium. Rice can be used to make everything from soups to salads, side dishes, entrees and desserts. It is also manufactured into cereal and flour, as well as a lactose-free milk alternative, which has only 1% fat.

Brown rice is whole-grain rice from which the outer husk has been removed. It is more nutritious than white rice and has a nutty flavor. Brown rice takes longer to cook than white rice. Although long-grain is the most common type of brown rice, it is also available in medium-and short-grain.

White rice is brown rice that has been stripped of its bran and germ. Due to the stripping process, white rice has fewer nutrients and less fiber than brown rice. The long-grain variety of white rice cooks into soft separate soft separate grains. If the package of rice says "enriched," rinsing or soaking the rice before cooking is not necessary. The rice has already been carefully washed and lightly coated with vitamins and minerals.

Converted rice is white rice that has been steamed before the bran is removed, which preserves some nutrients. The grains remain firmer than regular long-grain white rice, which makes it a good choice to add to long-cooking dishes, such as jambalaya, gumbo and paella.

Basmati rice is an aromatic white rice from India. Its long, tender grains have a distinct earthy aroma. It's great with curries or in pilafs.

Jasmine rice, like basmati, is a type of aromatic white rice with long, separate grains and a distinct perfumy aroma. The best is imported from Thailand. Domestically grown varieties are less aromatic.

Wehani red rice is a California medium-grained hybrid based on an Asian red rice variety. It has a chewy texture and an aroma similar to popcorn.

Arborio rice is a short-grained Italian variety that becomes creamy with constant stirring while cooking. It remains slightly firm after cooking, but absorbs the flavor of the cooking liquid. Arborio is a classic choice for making risotto.

ABOUT WILD RICE

Wild rice is not truly rice, but rather an aquatic grass native to North America. Originally it grew wild in the rivers and lakes of the northern Great Lakes region, but it's now mostly cultivated in that area, as well as in Minnesota and California. Wild rice has a very distinctive, nutty flavor and is delicious when combined with brown or white rice, or with lentils and other legumes. Dried fruits are particularly complementary to wild rice. Look for long, slender, uniformly shaped grains for salads and side dishes. Less expensive broken grains can be used for soups or stuffings.

BASIC COOKED BROWN RICE

MAKES 2⅓ CUPS

If you buy brown rice in bulk, sort through the grains, removing any little stones and other foreign material. Rinse the rice under several changes of cold water before proceeding.

2¼ cups water
1 cup long- or short-grain brown rice
1 tsp. salt

In a medium saucepan, bring water to a boil. Add rice and salt and cover pan tightly. Reduce heat to low and simmer for 30 to 45 minutes. Check a rice grain after 30 minutes to see if it is tender and water has been absorbed.

BASIC COOKED WHITE RICE

MAKES 3 CUPS

In general, basmati and Jasmine rice use a little less water than white rice, but the technique is the same. Unless the package or rice says "enriched," it is a good idea to rinse the rice under several changes of water until the water runs clear.

1¾–2 cups water
1 cup long- or medium-grain white rice
1 tsp. salt

Follow instructions for Basic Cooked Brown Rice, but cook white rice for 15 to 18 minutes; check a rice grain after 15 minutes.

BASIC COOKED WILD RICE

MAKES 4 CUPS

Rinse the wild rice to remove any loose hulls. Cooking in chicken stock adds richness and flavor. Wild rice can also be cooked in orange, apple, or tomato juice, particularly if it is going to be used in a salad. After draining, you can reserve the nutritious cooking liquid for soups or sauces.

3 cups water, chicken stock or other cooking liquid
½ tsp. salt
1 cup wild rice

In a large saucepan, bring water to a boil and add salt and rice. Reduce heat to low, cover and simmer for 40 to 45 minutes, until grains are tender and most have cracked open, exposing a fluffy white interior. Remove from heat and let stand covered for 10 minutes; drain if necessary.

RICE SOUP (CONGEE)

SERVES 4

Every rice-based cuisine has a version of this nourishing, easy-to-digest soup. It is often eaten as a late-night snack or for breakfast. Make a large batch of the basic soup and reheat it with different garnishes for weekday breakfasts. Or, add liquid to leftover cooked steamed rice and cook until it is very soft.

3½ cups Basic Chicken Stock, page 7,
   or canned chicken broth
3 cups water, plus more if needed for reheating
1 cup long- or medium-grain rice
Thin egg omelet, cut into strips for garnish,
   optional

Thinly sliced green onions or chopped fresh
   chives for garnish, optional
Diced cooked ham, chicken, or pork for garnish,
   optional
Soy sauce for garnish, optional
Hot pepper sauce for garnish; optional

In a heavy 4-quart saucepan, bring stock and water to a boil. Add rice and return to a boil. Stir mixture and reduce heat to very low. Partially cover pan and simmer slowly for 1½ hours, stirring occasionally. Serve immediately with desired garnishes or refrigerate. Mixture will thicken somewhat during cooling. Thin with a little more water or soy sauce when reheating.

BROWN RICE SALAD WITH TAHINI-LEMON DRESSING

SERVES 4 TO 6

Cool the rice before tossing it with the vegetables and dressing. Sesame tahini is available in Middle Eastern markets or in the ethnic food section of some major supermarkets.

1 yellow crookneck squash or zucchini, diced
½ cup diced carrot
½ cup diced roasted yellow or red bell pepper
4 green onions, white part only, minced
About 2 cups Basic Cooked Brown Rice, long-grain, page 36, cooled
2 Tbsp. chopped fresh parsley
5–6 fresh mint leaves, cut into ribbons

1½ Tbsp. lemon juice
1 Tbsp. rice vinegar
2 Tbsp. sesame tahini
1 Tbsp. olive oil
1 Tbsp. water
½ tsp. ground cumin
Salt and freshly ground pepper, to taste
5–6 drops Tabasco Sauce

Fill a medium saucepan with water and bring to a boil. Add squash and boil for 1 minute. Remove squash with a strainer and run under cold water to stop cooking. Add carrot to boiling water and boil for 2 minutes; drain and cool.

Place squash and carrot in a large bowl. Add pepper, onions, rice, parsley, and mint and mix well. In a small bowl, mix lemon juice, rice vinegar, sesame tahini, olive oil, water, cumin, salt, pepper, and Tabasco. Add dressing mixture to rice mixture and mix well. Serve immediately.

CLASSIC MUSHROOM PILAF

SERVES 4

Aromatic basmati rice is perfect for this side dish, but you can use another type of long-grain rice if you wish. Converted rice remains too firm and will not produce the desired texture for the pilaf. Start soaking the rice about 20 minutes before cooking the pilaf. The green peas can be cooked with the rice, or cooked separately and added just before serving to preserve their bright green color.

1 cup basmati or long-grain white rice
2 Tbsp. butter or ghee (clarified butter)
1 small onion, quartered and thinly sliced
5 large cremini (brown) or white mushrooms, trimmed and thinly sliced
1 small clove garlic, minced
¼ tsp. cardamom
1⅓ cups Basic Vegetable Stock, page 8, or canned vegetable broth
½ tsp. salt, to taste, or less if using canned broth
½ cup small green peas, thawed if frozen

Place rice in a medium bowl and rinse in several changes of cold water. When water runs clear, cover rice with cold water by about 1 inch and let stand for 30 minutes. Drain in a sieve and discard soaking liquid.

In a heavy saucepan with a tight-fitting lid, melt butter over medium heat until foaming. Add onion and sauté for 3 to 4 minutes. Add mushrooms and sauté for about 5 to 6 minutes, until mushroom liquid is released and are lightly browned. Add garlic and rice and sauté until rice is well coated with butter and grains begin to turn translucent. Add cardamom, stock and salt and bring to a boil. Stir in peas and return liquid to a boil. Cover pan, reduce heat to very low and simmer for 25 minutes. Do not remove lid during cooking time. Remove pan from heat and let stand covered for 5 minutes. Remove lid and gently fluff grains with a fork; serve immediately.

CLASSIC RISOTTO
SERVES 4

Risotto is typically made with the Italian short-grain rice called Arborio. A medium-grain California rice is an acceptable alternate. Use any of the stocks in the Basic Stocks chapter, or a good brand of canned chicken, beef, or vegetable broth.

2½–3 cups stock
2 Tbsp. full-flavored olive oil or butter or
   a combination
1 small onion, finely chopped
1 clove garlic, finely chopped

1 cup Arborio rice
Salt and freshly ground pepper, to taste
⅓ cup dry white wine or vermouth
3 Tbsp. finely chopped fresh parsley
Freshly grated Parmesan cheese

In a saucepan, bring stock to a boil over high heat. Reduce heat to very low and keep just at a simmer. In a heavy 2- to 3-quart saucepan, heat oil over medium heat. Add onion and sauté for 3 to 4 minutes. Add garlic and rice and sauté for about 2 minutes, until rice is well coated with oil and begins to turn translucent. Add salt and pepper. Combine wine with hot stock. Add about 1 cup of the simmering stock mixture to rice and cook, stirring until liquid is absorbed. Continue to add stock about ½ cup each time, stirring until rice has absorbed liquid before adding more. Rice should remain at a simmer. After rice has cooked for about 15 minutes, bite into a grain. It should be almost cooked through with just a small firm center; continue to cook, stirring, for 2 to 4 minutes, until center is soft, but not mushy. Check seasonings and serve immediately sprinkled with parsley. Pass Parmesan.

WARM SPINACH, MUSHROOM & BROWN RICE SALAD

SERVES 4

Cooked pearl barley or wheat rye or spelt berries can be substituted for the brown rice. The warm dressing should be poured over the salad just before serving.

4 slices bacon, cut into small pieces
2–3 Tbsp. olive oil
2 Tbsp. sherry vinegar
¼ cup dry vermouth or white wine
8 medium cremini (brown) mushrooms, trimmed and thinly sliced

⅓ cup finely chopped red onion
½ tsp. Dijon-style mustard
1 cup Basic Cooked Brown Rice, long grain, page 36
6 cups baby spinach leaves, well washed and dried
Salt and freshly ground pepper to taste

In a medium skillet, sauté bacon until brown and crisp. Remove bacon from pan and pour out drippings. To skillet, add olive oil, vinegar, and vermouth and bring to a boil over high heat. Add mushrooms and onion and cook over low heat for 3 to 4 minutes, until mushrooms and onion are soft. Add mustard and stir until well blended. Add rice and cook for 1 minute, until warmed. Place spinach leaves in a salad bowl and pour hot rice mixture over leaves. Toss, season with salt and pepper and serve immediately.

WILD RICE SALAD

SERVES 4

A piquant mustard dressing adds punch to a melange of wild rice, glazed shallots, raisins and almonds. Serve this as an accompaniment to grilled duck breasts or Cornish game hens.

2–3 large shallots
1 Tbsp. butter
1 Tbsp. sherry vinegar
1 Tbsp. lemon juice
1 quarter-sized piece fresh ginger, peeled and finely minced
½ tsp. sugar
2 tsp. Dijon-style mustard

¼ cup olive oil
Salt and freshly ground pepper, to taste
1 cup Basic Cooked Wild Rice, page 36, cooled
2 cups Basic Cooked White Rice (long-grain), page 36, cooled
⅓ cup slivered almonds or pine nuts, toasted
¼ cup raisins
2 Tbsp. chopped fresh parsley

Peel and trim shallots and cut into ¼-inch-thick slices widthwise. In a medium skillet, melt butter over medium heat and sauté shallots for 10 to 12 minutes, until tender and lightly browned. Remove from heat. In a small bowl, whisk together sherry vinegar, lemon juice, ginger, sugar, and mustard. Slowly add olive oil, whisking until well blended. Season with salt and pepper. Place rice in a serving bowl and mix with dressing. Add sautéed shallots, almonds, and raisins and toss lightly to combine. Stir in parsley and serve at room temperature.

WILD RICE PEPPER BOATS

SERVES 8

Colorful peppers are stuffed with a savory wild rice, mushroom, and cheese filling. Prepare the peppers early in the day and bake them just before serving.

4 large red or yellow bell peppers, cut in half lengthwise and seeded

2 Tbsp. full-flavored olive oil

1 cup finely chopped onion

8–10 cremini (brown) or shiitake mushrooms, coarsely chopped

2 cloves garlic, minced

Leaves from 2 sprigs fresh thyme

Pinch red pepper flakes

Salt and freshly ground pepper, to taste

½ cup chopped toasted walnuts

2 cups Basic Cooked Wild Rice, page 36

1 large egg, lightly beaten

¼ cup chopped sun-dried tomatoes

4 oz. feta cheese, crumbled, or 4 oz. smoked gouda, cut into ¼-inch cubes

Cook peppers in boiling water for 3 to 4 minutes, until peppers are softened, but still hold their shape; drain and cool. In a large skillet, heat oil over medium heat and sauté onion for 3 to 4 minutes. Add mushrooms and cook for 3 to 4 minutes, until they release their liquid. Add garlic, thyme, pepper flakes, salt, and pepper; cook for 1 to 2 minutes. Cool for 5 to 10 minutes and stir in walnuts, wild rice, egg, tomatoes, and cheese. Check seasonings. Heat oven to 350°F. Divide filling among peppers and place in an oiled baking pan with about ⅓ cup water. Bake stuffed peppers uncovered for 20 to 25 minutes until hot. Serve warm.

CORN & OATS

ABOUT CORN

Wild corn was domesticated by early residents of Central and South America long before the arrival of the Europeans. Most corn-growing tribes gave it almost god-like status, worshiping it in various ways. Native Americans taught European settlers to plant corn and it soon became a dietary staple.

Corn is a good source of carbohydrates and is high in B vitamins, potassium, and magnesium.

Cornmeal is made from dried, ground corn kernels. It comes in yellow, white or blue varieties, ground from yellow, white or blue corn kernels.

Polenta is a version of cornmeal made of both finely ground and coarsely ground cornmeal.

Corn flour is very finely ground cornmeal and is used in baking.

Grits are made from hominy, corn that has been soaked in wood ash or lye to loosen the outside hull and soften the kernel. There are many types of grits, some of which are made from untreated corn. Stone-ground grits have more flavor and texture than instant or quick-cooking grits.

ABOUT OATS

Oats have been cultivated since about the time of Christ. Oats, especially the bran, have received attention for their cholesterol-reducing properties. Oats have significant quantities of fiber, protein and trace minerals. Unlike many other grains, the oat germ, which contains oil, is not removed during processing; therefore, oats have a higher fat content than many other grains.

Rolled oats, also called old-fashioned oats, are made by slicing raw oats before steaming and "rolling" them into flakes.

Steel-cut oats, or Irish or Scotch oats, are whole-grain oats that have been coarsely sliced with sharp steel blades, which lends a chewy texture.

Quick-cooking oats are processed the same way as rolled oats, but they are rolled into very thin slices over a hot surface, which precooks them slightly.

Oat flour is made from finely ground oat groats. It has no gluten, so it must be used in conjunction with wheat flour in baking. In general, you can replace up to 25% of the wheat flour with oat flour in yeast breads and, depending on the recipe, up to 100% of the wheat flour in other baking recipes. Using oat flour lends a creamy, soft and moist texture to baked goods.

BASIC COOKED POLENTA

SERVES 4 TO 6

Starting the polenta in cold water helps to avoid lumps. Polenta doesn't need continuous attention, but should be stirred frequently to keep it from sticking to the bottom of your pot. For firm polenta, the mixture should be thick enough that a wooden spoon placed in the center will stand upright for 10 to 15 seconds.

4 cups cold water, Basic Chicken Stock, page 7, milk, or a combination
1 tsp. salt
1 cup coarse-ground polenta

2 Tbsp. butter, softened
Freshly ground black pepper, to taste
⅓ cup freshly grated Parmesan cheese
Butter or olive oil, optional

In a large, heavy saucepan, add cold water and salt. Stir in polenta. Place over high heat and stir until water comes to a boil. Reduce heat to low and simmer for 10 to 15 minutes, stirring every few minutes. Cook until polenta is soft and creamy and grains are soft. Stir in butter, pepper, and cheese. For soft polenta, serve immediately in a warmed large bowl or on a platter.

For firm polenta, transfer to a lightly oiled baking pan and spread to an even 9 x 9 x ½-inch square. Cover and refrigerate for at least 2 hours or overnight. Cut polenta into desired shapes, brush with melted butter or olive oil and reheat under the broiler or on a grill until golden brown. Or, sauté polenta shapes in a little butter until crisp and golden brown.

CORNMEAL & BUTTERMILK WAFFLES

MAKES EIGHT 6-INCH WAFFLES

Crisp, flavorful, and hearty, these cornmeal waffles can be mixed with a blender in less time than it takes to preheat the waffle iron. Bake the whole recipe and reheat the leftovers in the toaster for an easy breakfast on a busy morning. Or, serve hot waffles under creamed chicken or tuna for lunch or supper.

2 cups buttermilk
2 eggs
3 Tbsp. vegetable oil
1 tsp. salt
1 Tbsp. sugar

1¼ cups all-purpose flour
1 cup white, yellow, or blue cornmeal
¼ tsp. Tabasco Jalapeño Sauce, optional
1 tsp. baking soda

Heat waffle iron. In a blender, combine buttermilk, eggs, oil, salt, sugar, flour, cornmeal, and Tabasco, if using, and process on high speed for 1 minute. Scrape down the sides of blender if necessary. Add baking soda and pulse 2 to 3 times to combine. Spray waffle grids with nonstick cooking spray. Bake waffles according to manufacturer's instructions for your waffle iron.

CORNMEAL PIZZA CRUST

MAKES ONE 12-INCH CRUST, OR TWO 7-INCH CRUSTS

This toasty cornmeal crust makes a delicious base for your favorite pizza topping. Be sure to use bread flour in this recipe to achieve the right texture. A preheated pizza stone produces a wonderful crisp crust. Or, you can bake it in a deep pizza pan lined with parchment paper. To make a pizza: Heat oven to 425°F, spread the prebaked crust with your favorite topping and bake it for 12 to 15 minutes, until the topping is bubbling and the crust is golden.

1 cup warm water, about 105°F
1½ cups bread flour
1 pkg. active-dry yeast

3 Tbsp. olive oil
1 cup cornmeal or polenta
½ tsp. salt

Place water in the bowl of a heavy-duty mixer and stir in ½ cup of the flour and yeast. Let stand for about 15 minutes, until bubbling. Stir in olive oil and cornmeal and let stand for 10 minutes. Attach dough hook and, with mixer running, add salt and remaining 1 cup flour. Mix on medium speed for 6 minutes. Dough will be quite soft. Place a sheet of parchment paper or aluminum foil on a work surface. Lightly oil hands and press dough into a 12-inch circle on parchment or foil. Crimp edges to make a slight ridge. Lightly cover with plastic wrap or foil and let crust rise for about 30 minutes.

Heat oven to 325°F. Bake crust for about 20 minutes, until firm but not browned.

TACO-STYLE CORNMEAL PIZZA

SERVES 3 TO 4

Cooked taco filling with cheese and fresh salsa makes a zesty pizza. There will be a little taco meat left over that you can use as an omelet filling or in a quesadilla. Serve with a crisp green salad.

1 pkg. (1 oz.) taco seasoning mix
1 lb. lean ground beef
1 cup shredded mozzarella cheese
½ cup shredded sharp Cheddar cheese

1 prebaked Cornmeal Pizza Crust, page 52
1 cup prepared mild or hot chunky salsa
Fresh cilantro leaves for garnish

Heat oven to 425°F. Follow directions on taco seasoning mix for cooking beef. There should be no liquid remaining in skillet after cooking. Sprinkle cheeses evenly over crust and top with a generous portion of seasoned beef. Top with salsa. Bake for 12 to 15 minutes, until hot and bubbling. Cut into wedges and serve immediately garnished with cilantro.

SOUTHWESTERN CORN CAKES

MAKES 8

These piquant fresh corn cakes make a delicious side dish for grilled fish or chicken. If using a super-sweet variety of com, omit the sugar. Bake the cakes in nonstick muffin cups and time them to be done when the entrée is ready.

4 ears fresh white sweet corn, or 2 cups
    frozen white corn kernels
1 cup corn flour
¼ tsp. salt
¼ tsp. baking powder
¼ tsp. dry mustard

2 tsp. sugar
2 large eggs
⅓ cup milk
1 jalapeño chile, stemmed, seeded,
    and finely chopped
4 green onions, white part only, minced

Heat oven to 375°F. With a sharp knife, cut down the center of each row of corn kernels; cut corn from ears and set aside. Generously butter an 8-cup muffin tin. In a small bowl, combine flour, salt, baking powder, mustard, and sugar and stir well. In a medium bowl, whisk eggs with milk until frothy. Add flour mixture to egg mixture and whisk until smooth. Stir in corn, jalapeño, and onions. Pour about ⅓ cup batter into each muffin cup. Bake for 20 to 25 minutes, until cakes are puffy and golden brown. Serve immediately.

APPLE & OAT WAFFLES

MAKES SIX 6-INCH WAFFLES

Oat flour, rolled oats, and grated apple give an interesting texture to these fragrant waffles.

1½ cups oat flour
¼ cup regular rolled oats
1 tsp. cinnamon
2 tsp. baking powder
½ tsp. salt
2 large eggs

2 Tbsp. honey
1¼ cups milk
1 tsp. vanilla extract
1 medium Golden Delicious or Granny
   Smith apple, peeled and grated
3 Tbsp. butter, melted

Heat waffle iron. In a large bowl, stir together oat flour, rolled oats, cinnamon, baking powder, and salt. In another bowl, whisk eggs until frothy and beat in honey, milk, and vanilla. Pour egg mixture into flour mixture and stir just to combine. Fold in grated apple and melted butter. Spray waffle grids with nonstick cooking spray. Bake waffles according to manufacturer's instructions for your waffle iron.

HOT APPLE & STEEL-CUT OATS BREAKFAST

SERVES 6

Steel-cut oats have a chewier texture and more flavor than traditional rolled oats. Make this dish with apples or another favorite dried fruit before you go to bed. At breakfast time, spoon the mixture into a bowl and microwave it for a quick, nutritious breakfast. This can be refrigerated for up to a week.

2 cups apple juice
2 cups water
1 cup Irish steel-cut oats
¾ cup diced dried apples, apricots, peaches,
   or a mixture
1 Tbsp. brown sugar, plus more for serving,
   optional

1 Tbsp. butter, optional
¼ tsp. cinnamon
Dash freshly grated nutmeg
¼ tsp. salt
1 Tbsp. lemon juice
Milk for serving

In a medium saucepan, bring juice and water to a boil over high heat. Stir in oats, apples, brown sugar, butter, if using, cinnamon, nutmeg, and salt. Reduce heat to low and simmer uncovered for 30 minutes. Add lemon juice, ladle into cereal bowls and serve with milk and more sugar, if desired.

If making ahead, pour mixture into a covered container and refrigerate until ready to serve. Reheat in the microwave.

BANANA PECAN BREAD

MAKES 1 LOAF

Make this not-too-sweet bread when you have very ripe, soft bananas on hand. It tastes even better on the second day and is delicious toasted.

¼ cup butter, softened
1 cup sugar
2 eggs
1 cup mashed very ripe bananas
(about 2 medium)

2 cups oat flour
1 tsp. baking soda
½ tsp. salt
⅓ cup buttermilk
½ cup chopped pecans

Heat oven to 350°F. Oil a 9 x 5-inch loaf pan. With a mixer, beat butter and sugar until light and fluffy. Add eggs and bananas and mix well. In a small bowl, combine flour, baking soda, and salt and mix well. With mixer on low speed, mix flour mixture into egg mixture alternately with buttermilk. Continue mixing just until dry ingredients are combined. Fold in pecans. Spoon batter into prepared pan and bake for about 1 hour and 10 minutes, or until a toothpick inserted into the center comes out clean. Cool on a rack.

SUGAR & SPICE MUFFINS

MAKES 12

Mix up this muffin batter in the time it takes the oven to heat. Dip the baked muffins into cinnamon-sugar while still warm and watch them disappear.

½ cup butter, softened
1 cup sugar
1 egg
½ cup oat flour
1 cup all-purpose flour
2 tsp. baking powder

½ tsp. salt
¼ tsp. nutmeg
½ cup milk
1 tsp. cinnamon
⅓ cup butter, melted

Heat oven to 350°F. Butter a 12-cup muffin tin. With a mixer, beat ½ cup butter and ½ cup of the sugar until light and fluffy. Add egg and mix well. In a small bowl, mix together flours, baking powder, salt, and nutmeg. Gradually add flour mixture to butter mixture alternately with milk, mixing well after each addition. Distribute batter evenly in muffin cups. Bake for 20 to 25 minutes, until lightly browned and firm to the touch.

While muffins are baking, mix remaining ½ cup sugar with cinnamon. Remove hot muffins from pan. Dip top of each muffin into melted butter and then into sugar-cinnamon mixture. and serve.

PLUM CRISP WITH OATMEAL-WALNUT TOPPING

SERVES 8

This is the perfect finish for a summer dinner served warm or at room temperature. Top the crisp with a little whipped cream or vanilla ice cream if you like. Sliced peaches or nectarines can be substituted for the plums.

2 lb. fresh plums
¼ cup granulated sugar
Grated peel (zest) of 1 lemon
1 Tbsp. lemon juice
¼ tsp. salt
½ cup brown sugar, packed

1 tsp. cinnamon
½ cup oat flour or all-purpose flour
½ cup cold butter, cut into 12 pieces
½ cup regular rolled oats
½ cup chopped toasted walnuts

Heat oven to 350°F. Cut plums in half, remove and discard pits and cut fruit into ½-inch slices. Place fruit in a buttered 8 x 10-inch baking dish. Add granulated sugar, lemon zest, lemon juice, and ⅛ teaspoon of the salt and toss lightly to mix.

In a food processor, combine brown sugar, cinnamon, oat flour, and remaining ⅛ teaspoon salt and pulse 1 to 2 times. Add butter and pulse until butter mixture is the size of small peas. Transfer mixture to a bowl and stir in oats and walnuts. Distribute oat mixture evenly over fruit. Bake for 40 to 45 minutes, until fruit is bubbling and topping is nicely browned and crisp.

MILLET & BUCKWHEAT

ABOUT MILLET

Before written history, millet was widely grown in India, China and North Africa. Like barley, millet steadily declined in importance in many cultures as wheat and rice became more available. Although most consumers primarily think of it as a component of bird seed, cooked millet is delicious.

Millet is gluten-free, which makes it a good grain for people who are allergic to wheat. Millet is also rich in fiber and protein. Millet cooks in about the same time as white rice and can be substituted for it in many rice recipes. Try millet in soups, salads and main courses.

Hulled millet seeds are whole-grain millet from which the indigestible outer hull has been removed.

Millet flour is made from ground millet seeds. It has a slightly sweet flavor. Up to 10% of the wheat flour in bread recipes can be replaced by millet flour.

Puffed millet is a popular breakfast cereal and can be used for a crunchy topping for baked goods. It is similar to puffed rice and puffed wheat. Look for it in boxes in the cereal aisle of the supermarket or in bulk bins.

ABOUT BUCKWHEAT

Buckwheat is not a true grain, but is treated as such in cooking. Buckwheat is related to the rhubarb family and probably originated in Asia, where it has been grown for at least a thousand years. Buckwheat was introduced into Europe in the Middle Ages and became an important food resource in Russia, northern Italy and parts of France.

Buckwheat is high in protein, potassium and phosphorus and has a distinctive, somewhat earthy taste. It is versatile and comes in many forms.

Kasha is the familiar name for roasted buckwheat goats or kernels. Kasha is a quick-cooking grain that can be cooked in milk for a nutritious hot breakfast cereal or cooked in water or stock for pilafs or salads.

Buckwheat flour, made from ground buckwheat seeds, has a pronounced flavor. Buckwheat flour is most often used in blinis (tiny Russian-style savory pancakes) and breakfast pancakes.

Soba are Japanese-style noodles made from buckwheat and wheat flour. Soba can be used in much the same way as wheat pasta.

BASIC COOKED MILLET

MAKES 3½ CUPS

Hulled millet is more flavorful when it is toasted before cooking.

¾ cup hulled millet seeds
2 cups water or stock
¼ tsp. salt

To toast millet, place in a heavy skillet and cook over medium-high heat, stirring constantly, for 4 to 5 minutes, or until millet is lightly browned and has a toasty aroma. Remove from heat.

To cook millet, pour toasted millet into a large saucepan. Add water and salt and bring to a boil over high heat. Cover pan, reduce heat to low and simmer for about 20 minutes, until most of the water has been absorbed. Remove from heat and let stand for 10 minutes. Remove lid and fluff grains with a fork. Cool to room temperature before refrigerating. Keeps covered for 2 to 3 days in the refrigerator.

BASIC COOKED KASHA (ROASTED BUCKWHEAT GROATS)

MAKES 3½ CUPS

There are two kinds of kasha: a lightly roasted type and a darker roasted version, with a more assertive flavor. Coating the kasha with egg before cooking produces individual grains after cooking. Cooking kasha in broth adds flavor.

2 cups water or stock
Salt (if not using canned broth)
1 large egg, lightly beaten
1 cup kasha

In a large saucepan, bring water to a boil. Add salt, if using. In a bowl, combine egg and kasha and stir to thoroughly coat kasha with egg. Heat a heavy nonstick skillet over medium heat and stir-fry kasha for 3 to 4 minutes, until kasha grains separate, stirring to break up any clumps. Immediately pour kasha grains into boiling water, cover, reduce heat to low and simmer for 8 to 10 minutes, until kasha is tender. Remove kasha from heat and drain, if necessary. Fluff grains with a fork and cool.

MILLET-STUFFED ARTICHOKES

SERVES 4

Use a grapefruit spoon or melon bailer to scrape out each prickly "choke" before filling the artichokes with this savory herb stuffing.

Juice of 1 lemon
4 medium artichokes (about 8 oz. each)
3 Tbsp. full-flavored olive oil
1 cup fresh breadcrumbs
2 cloves garlic, finely chopped
1 cup Basic Cooked Millet, page 63

1 Tbsp. finely chopped fresh parsley
1 Tbsp. finely chopped fresh mint
2 Tbsp. white wine vinegar or lemon juice
2 Tbsp. pine nuts, toasted
¼ cup freshly grated Parmesan cheese
Salt and freshly ground pepper, to taste

Fill a large bowl with cold water and add lemon juice. Wash artichokes and cut stems flush with bottoms to make flat bases. With a large knife, cut straight across the top of artichokes about 1 inch down. Remove 2 or 3 layers of outer leaves and trim rough edges of artichoke bottom where leaves were removed. Gently spread artichoke leaves and, using a sharp spoon or melon baller, remove prickly center leaves. Scrape out as much of the fuzzy choke as possible and discard. Immediately place trimmed artichokes in lemon water.

In a large skillet, heat 2 tablespooons of the olive oil over medium heat. Add breadcrumbs and sauté until lightly browned and crisp. Add garlic and sauté for 30 seconds; remove from heat. Transfer breadcrumb mixture to a medium bowl. Add millet, parsley, mint, vinegar, pine nuts, Parmesan cheese, salt, and pepper and mix well.

Drain artichokes up-side down on paper towels for 2 to 3 minutes. Using about ¼ of the stuffing for each artichoke, spoon some filling into the center of artichoke. Repeat with remaining artichokes and filling. As artichokes are stuffed, place them in a pot with a tight-fitting lid just large enough to hold them. To pot, add water to a depth of 1 inch. Drizzle remaining 1 tablespoon olive oil over artichokes. Cover pot and bring water just to a boil over high heat. Immediately reduce heat to low and simmer for 40 to 45 minutes, until each artichoke base is tender when pierced with a knife. Check occasionally to see if additional water is needed. Serve warm or at room temperature.

TUNA MILLET SALAD

SERVES 2 TO 3

This salad travels well and makes great lunchbox or picnic fare. Roll it up in lettuce leaves or spoon it into radicchio cups for an attractive presentation. This recipe doubles easily.

1 cup Basic Cooked Millet, page 63
1 can (6½ oz.) water- or oil-packed tuna,*
    drained
⅓ cup finely chopped celery
1 medium tomato, peeled, seeded and
    chopped (about ½ cup)
2 Tbsp. finely chopped green onions or fresh chives

¼ cup chopped fresh parsley
¼ tsp. Tabasco Jalapeño Sauce
Salt and freshly ground pepper, to taste
2 Tbsp. buttermilk
1 Tbsp. lemon juice
2 tsp. full-flavored olive oil
Butter lettuce or radicchio leaves, optional

In a medium bowl, combine millet, tuna, celery, tomato, onions, and parsley and lightly toss together. Stir in Tabasco, salt, and pepper. Stir in buttermilk, lemon juice, and olive oil. Adjust seasonings. Serve immediately spooned into lettuce or radicchio leaves, if desired. Refrigerate for up to 2 days. Bring to room temperature before serving.

*Note: If using oil-packed tuna. reduce olive oil to 1 teaspoon.

CURRIED LENTILS & MILLET

SERVES 4 TO 6

This savory vegetarian side dish is satisfying for lunch or supper when accompanied by a green salad. Or, serve it with roasted chicken or pork. Check lentils for stones or other materials that may have slipped through during processing.

3 Tbsp. vegetable oil
1 large yellow onion, chopped
1 small carrot, coarsely grated
1 jalapeño chile, stemmed, seeded, and finely minced
1 Tbsp. curry powder
½ cup toasted millet (see page 63)
1 cup brown lentils, rinsed

3½ cups Basic Vegetable Stock, page 8, or canned vegetable broth
Salt and freshly ground pepper, to taste
Hot pepper sauce to taste, optional
¼ cup chopped fresh cilantro
¼ cup chopped fresh mint
Plain yogurt for garnish, optional

In a heavy 3½- to 4-quart pot, heat oil over medium-low heat. Add onion and sauté for 5 to 7 minutes, until soft and translucent. Add carrot, jalapeño, and curry powder and sauté for 1 minute, or until curry powder is fragrant. Add millet and stir to coat well. Add lentils and stock and bring to a boil over high heat. Partially cover pot, reduce heat to low and simmer for 35 to 45 minutes, until lentils are tender. Stir in salt, pepper, and hot pepper sauce. Sprinkle with cilantro and mint and top with dollops of yogurt, if desired. Serve hot.

SPINACH-MILLET GNOCCHI

SERVES 4 TO 6

Allow time for the gnocchi mixture to chill in the refrigerator before cooking.

¼ cup butter
¼ cup minced shallots or onion
1 large clove garlic, finely chopped
1 pkg. (10 oz.) frozen chopped spinach, thawed and squeezed very dry
1 cup Basic Cooked Millet, page 63
⅓ cup ricotta cheese

1 large egg, lightly beaten
⅓ cup flour
⅓ cup freshly grated Parmesan cheese
Pinch nutmeg
Salt and freshly ground pepper, to taste
1 Tbsp. salt

In a medium skillet, melt 2 tabelspoons of the butter over medium-low heat. Add shallots and sauté for 2 to 3 minutes; add garlic and sauté for 1 minute. Add spinach and millet and sauté for 4 to 5 minutes, until moisture has evaporated and mixture is dry. Remove skillet from heat, transfer spinach mixture to a bowl and cool for 10 minutes. To bowl, add ricotta, egg, flour, ¼ cup of the Parmesan, nutmeg, salt, and pepper and mix well. Cover mixture and refrigerate until very firm, about 1 hour.

In a large shallow saucepan, bring about 2½ quarts water to a boil over high heat. Add 1 tablespoon salt and reduce heat to low. Shape gnocchi mixture into small balls about 1½ inches in diameter. Gently drop gnocchi into simmering water, 8 to 10 at a time, and cook for 7 to 8 minutes, until gnocchi float and are slightly firm to the touch. Carefully remove gnocchi with a slotted spoon and drain on paper towels. If some have ragged edges or fall apart, gently reshape when cool enough to handle. Drizzle with remaining 1 tablespoon butter and sprinkle with remaining Parmesan cheese.

BUCKWHEAT CORN PANCAKES

MAKES EIGHTEEN 5-INCH PANCAKES

Tender and flavorful—these pancakes go together quickly and are delicious smothered in maple syrup. Or, make miniature pancakes and serve them with smoked salmon and sour cream to accompany champagne. Baked pancakes will keep for several days in the refrigerator or longer in the freezer. To serve, place on serving plate, drizzle with a little syrup, cover and reheat briefly in the microwave.

2 cups buttermilk
2 large eggs
¼ cup canola oil
¾ tsp. salt
½ cup buckwheat flour

½ cup corn flour
½ cup all-purpose flour
2 tsp. baking soda
Maple syrup or honey for serving

In a bowl, combine buttermilk, eggs, oil, and salt and whisk until well blended. In another bowl, stir together flours and baking soda. Add flour mixture to buttermilk mixture and whisk until just combined.

Heat a griddle or large skillet over medium heat. When hot, wipe skillet with an oil-saturated paper towel. For each pancake, spoon about 3 tablespoons of the batter on griddle. When large holes form in batter, flip pancakes with a spatula. Cook pancakes briefly on second side. Serve on warm plates with maple syrup or honey.

COLD SOBA NOODLE SALAD

SERVES 4

Serve this colorful Asian-style salad as the main attraction for a light lunch. Or, serve it as an appetizing addition to a picnic or buffet.

5 dried shiitake mushrooms
1 cup hot water
4 oz. snow peas (about 15)
¼ red or green bell pepper, cut into thin strips
5 green onions, white part only, thinly sliced
½ cup coarsely grated carrot
6 oz. soba noodles
1 Tbsp. salt

1 Tbsp. Dijon-style mustard
1 Tbsp. soy sauce or tamari
2 Tbsp. rice vinegar
1 tsp. grated fresh ginger
1 Tbsp. vegetable oil
1 tsp. toasted sesame oil
Salt and white pepper, to taste

Place mushrooms in a small bowl, cover with hot water and let stand for 20 minutes, until softened. Drain mushrooms, remove and discard stems and cut mushrooms into thin strips. Cook snow peas in boiling water for 30 seconds. Drain snow peas and cut lengthwise into thin strips.

Bring a large pot of water to a boil. Add salt and stir in noodles. Cook noodles according to package directions, until cooked through, but still slightly firm to the bite (*al dente*).

While noodles are cooking, combine mustard, soy sauce, vinegar and grated ginger in a large salad bowl. Slowly add vegetable and sesame oils, whisking until dressing thickens.

Drain cooked noodles well and pour into bowl with dressing. Toss to coat noodles with dressing and season with salt and pepper. Add mushrooms and vegetables and toss again. Serve at room temperature.

KASHA-CARROT SALAD WITH MUSTARD DRESSING

SERVES 4

Cooking the diced carrots ahead of time makes this a quick salad to put together. This salad can be refrigerated for several hours, but bring it to room temperature before serving.

2 cups cooled Basic Cooked Kasha, page 63
2 cups diced cooked carrots, ⅜-inch dice
Salt and freshly ground pepper, to taste
3 Tbsp. olive oil
1 Tbsp. rice vinegar
2 Tbsp. lemon juice
4 tsp. Dijon-style mustard

½ tsp. sugar
1 tsp. sesame oil
½ tsp. grated fresh ginger
Red pepper flakes to taste
¼ cup fresh cilantro leaves, packed
2 Tbsp. chopped fresh parsley

In a medium bowl, combine kasha and carrots. Season with salt and pepper and mix well. In a blender or food processor, combine olive oil, vinegar, lemon juice, mustard, sugar, sesame oil, ginger, pepper flakes, and cilantro leaves. Process until mixture is creamy. Pour dressing over kasha mixture and mix well. Check seasonings. Add chopped parsley and toss well.

QUINOA & AMARANTH

ABOUT QUINOA & AMARANTH

Quinoa and amaranth are highly nutritious, containing balanced protein, calcium and other minerals.

Quinoa (pronounced "KEEN-wah") was a staple food of the Incas for thousands of years. After their arrival, the Spaniards encouraged the cultivation of other grains with a higher yield, thus quinoa diminished in importance. Quinoa has recently experienced a resurgence in popularity, particularly for those on gluten-free diets.

Quinoa is not a "true" grain because it has balanced amino acids. It is considered to have a higher protein content than any grain. While growing, individual grains of quinoa are covered with a natural, bitter-tasting coating, which protects it from insects and birds. Commercially available quinoa has been washed, but it is still a good idea to rinse the grains well before cooking.

Whole-grain quinoa has a mild, delicate flavor and a slightly crunchy texture. The cooked grains are almost translucent. Cooked quinoa can substitute for rice in dishes and, like rice, it serves as a foil for strong flavors.

Quinoa flour is made from ground quinoa grains. It lends a distinct flavor to baked goods and is made into pasta. In general, you can replace up to 25% of the wheat flour with quinoa flour in yeast breads.

The Aztecs believed amaranth to be as important as corn and beans for food. Vital to their culture, it provided energy for making superior warriors. With the death of Montezuma, Cortez commanded that the grain fields be burned. Amaranth was relegated to a minor status in the New World and never established a foothold in Europe. Rediscovered in '70s, amaranth is becoming more widely grown and available.

Amaranth is rich in protein, lysine, and calcium and other minerals. It has an aroma and flavor that reminds some people of celery.

Whole-grain amaranth has a tendency to stick together, making it an ideal fat-free thickener for soups and sauces. Cooked amaranth quickly becomes quite firm upon cooling, but it can easily be reconstituted in the microwave.

Amaranth flour is made from ground amaranth seeds. In general, you can replace up to 25% of the wheat flour with amaranth flour in yeast breads.

Amaranth flakes make a good breakfast cereal and are perfect to use as a crunchy topping for a casserole.

BASIC COOKED QUINOA

MAKES 3½ TO 4 CUPS

Toasting quinoa yields a richer flavor. If the recipe calls for toasted quinoa, place rinsed grains in a skillet over medium-high heat and stir until grains turn a darker shade of brown and smell toasted.

1 cup quinoa, rinsed
2 cups water or stock
Pinch salt

Place quinoa in a sieve and rinse well under cold running water. Transfer to a medium saucepan with water and salt and bring to a boil over high heat. Cover pan, reduce heat to low and simmer for 10 to 15 minutes, until grains are translucent and the outer germ separates from grain. Drain any excess water and cool.

BASIC COOKED AMARANTH

MAKES 2 CUPS

Amaranth cooks into a thick, creamy mixture, which is delicious in soups and stews. Cooked amaranth can be thinned to the desired consistency with water.

1 cup amaranth
3 cups cold water or stock
Pinch salt

Place amaranth in a medium saucepan with water and salt and bring to a boil over high heat. Cover pan, reduce heat to low and simmer for 25 minutes, until grains are tender and liquid has been absorbed.

AMARANTH-APPLESAUCE MUFFINS

MAKES 12

Applesauce adds flavor and gives these easy-to-put-together muffins a tender, moist texture.

¼ cup butter, softened
½ cup brown sugar, packed
1 large egg
1 cup applesauce
1 cup all-purpose flour
1 cup amaranth flour

2 tsp. baking powder
½ tsp. salt
1 tsp. cinnamon
¼ tsp. nutmeg
¼ tsp. ground cloves
½ cup raisins

Heat oven to 400°F. Butter a 12-cup muffin tin and set aside. With a mixer, beat butter and sugar until light and fluffy. Add egg and beat well. Stir in applesauce. In another bowl, sift together flours, baking powder, salt, cinnamon, nutmeg, and cloves. Add flour mixture to applesauce mixture and stir just to moisten dry ingredients. Fold in raisins, taking care not to overmix batter. Spoon batter into muffin cups. Bake for 18 to 20 minutes, until a toothpick inserted into the center of a muffin comes out clean.

QUINOA PECAN WAFFLES

MAKES SEVEN TO EIGHT 6-INCH WAFFLES

Cooked quinoa and chopped pecans add interesting flavor and texture to these crispy waffles.

¾ cup all-purpose flour
½ cup corn flour or rice flour
2 tsp. baking soda
1 tsp. baking powder
½ tsp. salt
3 large eggs, separated

3 Tbsp. vegetable oil
1 Tbsp. honey
2 cups buttermilk
1 cup Basic Cooked Quinoa, page 75
⅓ cup chopped pecans

Heat waffle iron. In a large bowl, combine flours, soda, baking powder, and salt and stir well. In a small bowl, whisk egg yolks until lemon-colored and stir in oil, honey, and buttermilk. Pour egg mixture into flour mixture and stir just to combine. Stir in quinoa and pecans. In another bowl, beat egg whites until stiff peaks form and fold into batter. Spray waffle grids with nonstick cooking spray. Bake waffles according to manufacturer's instructions for your waffle iron.

QUINOA, CARROT & TAHINI DIP

MAKES 3 CUPS

Scoop up this full-flavored dip with pita chips or pieces of carrot, turnip, jicama, or celery. The dip keeps well in the refrigerator for a few days.

1¼ cups water
½ cup quinoa, rinsed
2 carrots, peeled and coarsely grated
4 cloves roasted garlic
¼ cup tahini or Asian sesame paste
¼ cup lemon juice
½ tsp. ground cumin

2–3 drops Tabasco Sauce, optional
¼ tsp. salt
Freshly ground pepper to taste
1–2 Tbsp. water, if needed
Paprika for garnish
Chopped fresh cilantro or parsley for garnish

In a medium saucepan, bring water to a boil. In a dry skillet, toast quinoa over medium heat for 3 to 4 minutes, until lightly browned. Transfer quinoa with carrots to pan with boiling water. Cover pan, reduce heat to low and simmer for 18 minutes, until quinoa is soft and liquid has been absorbed. Remove from heat and let stand covered for a few minutes. Transfer mixture to a food processor and process until smooth. Add garlic, tahini, lemon juice, cumin, Tabasco, salt, and pepper and pulse several times to blend well. Adjust seasonings and transfer to a serving bowl. Chill mixture until about 30 minutes before serving. Thin with 1 to 2 tablespoons water, if needed, to reach dipping consistency. Garnish with paprika and cilantro.

CREAMY CORN & QUINOA SOUP

SERVES 4

Make this soup the day before you serve it and present it as a first course for a summer dinner party. For a different accent garnish it with fresh cilantro and thin lime slices, or dollops of fresh tomato and avocado salsa. Amaranth or millet can be substituted for the quinoa.

1 Tbsp. vegetable oil
1 cup diced onion
1 large jalapeño chile, stemmed, seeded and minced
Kernels from 4 large ears fresh sweet corn, or 2 pkg. (10 oz. each) frozen corn
3 cups water
3 cups Basic Chicken Stock, page 7, or canned chicken broth
½ cup quinoa, rinsed
Salt and freshly ground pepper, to taste
2 Tbsp. fresh lime juice
1 Tbsp. butter
Sweet basil leaves, cut into ribbons for garnish

In a stockpot, heat oil over medium heat. Add onion and jalapeño and sauté for 3 to 4 minutes. Reserve ½ cup corn kernels for garnish. Add remaining corn to skillet and cook for 2 to 3 minutes. Add water and bring to a boil over high heat. Cover pot, reduce heat to low and simmer for 20 minutes, until vegetables are tender. Remove pot from heat and cool for a few minutes.

Process vegetables with a food processor and strain through a coarse sieve. Return smooth vegetable mixture to stockpot, add chicken stock and bring to a boil over high heat. Stir in quinoa, salt, and pepper. Reduce heat to low and simmer for 20 minutes, until quinoa is translucent. Add lime juice and adjust seasonings.

In a small saucepan, heat butter over medium-low heat and sauté reserved ½ cup corn kernels for 3 to 4 minutes, until tender. Ladle soup into warm bowls and garnish each serving with a spoonful of sautéed corn and a few ribbons of basil. Serve immediately.

LEEK, POTATO & AMARANTH SOUP

SERVES 8 TO 10

It takes less than an hour to make this soup. Use the thin slicing blade on the food processor to slice the potatoes.

3 Tbsp. butter
3 large leeks, white part only, well washed
   and coarsely chopped (about 4 cups)
2 medium stalks celery, thinly sliced
½ cup amaranth
2–3 cups sliced peeled potatoes
   (about 2 large, or 1½ lb.)

4 cups Basic Chicken Stock, page 7, or
   canned chicken broth
3 cups water
Salt and finely ground white pepper, to taste
Chopped fresh parsley or chives for garnish

In a large heavy stockpot, melt butter over medium heat. Add leeks and celery and sauté for 5 to 6 minutes, until softened. Stir in amaranth. Add sliced potatoes, chicken stock, and water and bring to a boil over high heat. Cover pot, reduce heat to low and simmer for about 40 minutes. Cool soup for a few minutes. With a food processor or blender, carefully purée hot soup in batches and return to pot. Season with salt and pepper, heat through and garnish with chopped parsley.

QUINOA SALAD WITH ROASTED CORN, MANGO & BLACK BEANS

SERVES 4 TO 6

This colorful salad boasts a lively curry and lime vinaigrette. Serve it as an accompaniment to grilled meats or as part of a salad buffet. Substitute couscous or kasha for the quinoa, if you like.

Kernels from 3 ears fresh sweet corn (about 2 cups)
5 Tbsp. vegetable oil
Salt and freshly ground pepper, to taste
½ cup finely chopped red onion
1 jalapeño chile, stemmed, seeded, and minced

1 tsp. Madras curry powder
1½ cups Basic Cooked Quinoa, page 75
1 can (15 oz.) black beans, rinsed and drained
1 ripe mango, peeled and diced
1 lime

Heat oven to 425°F. Line a rimmed baking sheet with foil. Toss corn with 2 Tbsp. of the oil, salt, and pepper and spread in a single layer on baking sheet. Bake for 15 to 18 minutes, stirring once or twice, until corn is lightly browned; cool slightly. In a small skillet, heat remaining 3 tablespoons vegetable oil over low heat. Add onion and jalapeño and sauté for 4 to 5 minutes, until onion is soft and translucent. Stir in curry powder and cook for 1 minute. In a bowl, combine roasted corn, onion mixture, quinoa, beans, and mango. Squeeze lime juice over salad and season with salt and pepper.

KAMUT, RYE, TRITICALE & FLAX

ABOUT KAMUT, RYE, TRITICALE & FLAX

Many unusual grains are available in specialty markets and health food stores, and provide interesting and healthful additions to our daily diet.

Kamut (pronounced "kah-MOOT") is an ancient Egyptian form of wheat with kernels 2 to 3 times larger than regular wheat. Although kamut does contain gluten, some people who are sensitive to wheat can eat it.

Whole-grain kamut can be substituted for wheat berries in most recipes.

Kamut flakes, a cereal form of kamut, can be used in baking or for a crispy topping for a gratin or casserole.

Rye can be grown in cold, damp climates where wheat does not grow well, such as Russia, Scandinavia and Eastern Europe. Rye has a slight gray hue and tangy taste.

Rye berries can be substituted for wheat, spelt or triticale berries in recipes.

Rye flour, commonly used in pumpernickel and rye breads, contains little gluten. In general, you can replace up to 50% of the wheat flour with rye flour in yeast breads to make nice, light breads with good rye flavor.

Triticale (pronounced "tri-ti-CAY-lee") is a cross between wheat and rye that thrives in cold, damp climates where wheat doesn't grow well.

Triticale berries are similar to wheat berries, only smaller. You can substitute triticale berries for wheat berries, rye berries, brown rice or pearl barley in recipes.

Triticale flour has a small amount of gluten which, if using exclusively in bread recipes, requires more gentle kneading and only one rising period.

Flax has been cultivated to make linen fiber since the time of the Egyptian mummies. Today, a second strain of flax is produced for oil and food. Research suggests that flax may provide beneficial nutrients. Flax provides soluble fiber, Omega-3 fatty acids and high-quality protein. Use caution when using flax in cooking as, like wheat and other grains, some people are allergic to it. Flax is used for baked goods and crackers or it can be added to cooked vegetable dishes or grain salads.

Whole flaxseed can be ground in a coffee or spice mill as you need it.

Milled flaxseed is available, but doesn't keep as long as whole flaxseed. Store milled flaxseed in the refrigerator and use within a few days.

BASIC COOKED KAMUT

MAKES 3 CUPS

Do not add salt to kamut while cooking; doing so could increase the cooking time and/or toughen the grains.

1 cup kamut
3 cups cold water, plus water to cover

Place kamut in a medium saucepan and cover with water; cover pan and let stand for 6 to 8 hours, or overnight. *Quick Soak Method*: Place kamut in a medium saucepan, cover with water and bring to a boil. Cover pan, remove from heat and let stand for 1 hour; drain.

In a saucepan, bring 3 cups cold water to a boil over high heat. Add soaked kamut. Cover pan, reduce heat to low and simmer for 45 to 50 minutes, until kamut is tender.

BASIC COOKED RYE OR TRITICALE BERRIES

MAKES 2 TO 2½ CUPS

Rye berries and triticale berries are very sturdy and require lengthy cooking times. If buying berries in bulk, carefully sort through them to remove any small stones or debris. Rinse rye or triticale berries well in cold water before using. Do not salt the berries until after they are cooked, as salt slows down the absorption of liquid into the grain.

1 cup rye or triticale berries
3 cups cold water, plus water to cover

Place rye or triticale berries in a large bowl and cover with cold water. Let stand covered overnight; drain. *Quick Soak Method*: Place berries in a medium saucepan, cover with water and bring to a boil. Remove from heat and let stand for 1 hour; drain.

In a medium saucepan, bring 3 cups water to a boil over high heat. Add soaked rye or triticale berries. Reduce heat to low, cover pan and simmer for about 30 to 45 minutes, until tender.

CRANBERRY BATTER BREAD

SERVES 8

This slightly sweet bread features dried cranberries and nuts. Serve it warm, at room temperature or cut into slices and toasted. This bread freezes well.

⅓ cup organic triticale, wheat, or amaranth flakes
1 cup kamut flour
2¼ cups all-purpose flour
½ tsp. cinnamon
½ tsp. mace
1 tsp. salt
½ cup sugar

1½ tsp. baking powder
¼ cup butter, cut into 4 pieces
1¾ cups milk
2 large eggs, lightly beaten
1 tsp. vanilla extract
1 cup dried cranberries
1 cup chopped toasted walnuts

Heat oven to 350°F. Butter an 8 x 8 x 2½-inch pan and set aside. In a large bowl, combine triticale flakes, flours, cinnamon, mace, salt, sugar, and baking powder and stir until mixed. In a small saucepan, heat butter and milk over medium heat until butter melts. Pour hot milk mixture into flour mixture and stir until mixed. Add eggs and vanilla and mix well. Stir in cranberries and walnuts, taking care not to overmix batter. Spoon batter into prepared baking pan. Bake for 55 to 60 minutes, until top is lightly browned and a toothpick inserted into the center comes out clean. Cool on a rack.

KAMUT & BEAN SOUP

SERVES 4

Traditional flavors of Mexico complement this hearty soup. If you like, add some diced cooked chicken at the very end and cook the soup for another 5 minutes. You can substitute cooked wheat berries or rye berries for kamut if desired.

2 Tbsp. vegetable oil
1 large onion, finely chopped
2 carrots, peeled and finely diced
2 cloves garlic, finely chopped
1 canned chipotle chile, stemmed, seeded,
    and finely chopped
½ tsp. dried oregano
1 tsp. ground cumin
2 cups Basic Cooked Kamut, page 87

1 can (14 oz.) ready-cut tomatoes
2½ cups Basic Chicken Stock, page 7, or
    canned chicken broth
Salt and freshly ground pepper, to taste
1 can (15 oz.) pinto beans, rinsed and drained
1 Tbsp. lime juice
Fresh cilantro leaves for garnish
1 cup shredded Monterey Jack cheese for garnish
Lime wedges

In a heavy 3-quart saucepan, heat oil over medium-low heat and sauté onion and carrots for 8 to 10 minutes, until soft. Add garlic, chipotle, oregano, and cumin and cook for 2 to 3 minutes. Add kamut and toss to coat well. Add tomatoes, stock, salt, and pepper and bring to a boil over high heat. Reduce heat to low and simmer uncovered for 15 minutes. Add beans and heat through. Stir in lime juice. Serve in warm soup bowls garnished with cilantro. Pass cheese and limes.

CARAMELIZED ONION & POTATO GRATIN

SERVES 4 TO 6

The potatoes can be boiled or baked for this gratin, which can be assembled ahead of time and baked just before serving. Kamut flakes provide a wonderful crunch to the crispy topping.

2 lb. Yukon gold or russet potatoes, cooked and peeled
1 cup buttermilk
Salt and freshly ground pepper, to taste

2 Tbsp. full-flavored olive oil
1 large onion, coarsely chopped
¾ cup kamut flakes
2 Tbsp. freshly grated Parmesan cheese

Mash cooked potatoes or run through a ricer. Place mashed potatoes in a bowl and gradually add buttermilk, beating until smooth. Season with salt and pepper. In a medium skillet, heat olive oil over medium-low heat and sauté onion for 10 to 15 minutes, until lightly browned and soft. Add kamut flakes and Parmesan cheese and toss to thoroughly mix with onion and olive oil.

Heat oven to 375°F. Oil a 8 x 8-inch baking pan. Spread potato mixture evenly in pan and top with kamut-onion mixture. Bake for 25 to 30 minutes, until potatoes are heated through and topping is lightly browned. Serve hot.

ONION TART WITH RYE CRUST

SERVES 6

Sweet "melted" onions and tangy cheese fill a savory rye crust. Serve wedges of this tart with lightly dressed salad greens on the side. Make the pastry first and cook the onions while the pastry is chilling.

¾ cup all-purpose flour
½ cup rye flour
½ tsp, salt
6 Tbsp. chilled butter, cut into 6 pieces

2 Tbsp. plain yogurt or sour cream
1–2 Tbsp. ice water
Onion Filling, recipe follows on facing page

In a food processor, combine flours and salt. Add butter and pulse 6 or 7 times, until butter is size of small peas. Add yogurt and 1 tablespoon ice water. Process until mixture starts to form a ball, adding additional water if dough is too dry to hold together. Form dough into a flat round, wrap in plastic wrap and refrigerate for 1 hour.

Heat oven to 400°F. Place dough between 2 sheets of waxed paper and roll out to a 12-inch circle. Place in a 9 x 2½-inch tart pan with a removable bottom, allowing dough to come up the sides. Cover dough with aluminum foil and fill with pie weights or dried beans. Bake for 15 minutes. Remove foil and weights and continue to bake for 2 to 3 minutes, until crust feels dry to the touch. Cool on a rack.

Pour *Onion Filling* into cooled crust. Reduce oven temperature to 375°F and bake tart for about 1 hour, until filling is puffed and lightly browned. Serve warm or at room temperature.

ONION FILLING

3 large onions, about 1½ lb.
2 Tbsp. butter
½ tsp. dried thyme
¼ cup dry vermouth

1 Tbsp. balsamic vinegar
4 large eggs
⅔ cup shredded Gruyère cheese
Salt and freshly ground pepper, to taste

Peel onions, cut into quarters and thinly slice crosswise. In a large skillet over medium heat, melt butter. Add sliced onions and sauté for 5 to 6 minutes, taking care not to let onions brown. Add thyme and vermouth. Cover pan and cook over very low heat for 25 to 30 minutes, stirring once or twice, until onions are very soft. If onions start to stick to pan, add a little water. Remove lid, increase heat to medium and cook until any liquid in pan has evaporated. Stir in balsamic vinegar and remove from heat. Cool for at least 5 minutes. In a large bowl, whisk eggs. Stir in grated cheese and onions. Season mixture with salt and pepper.

WALNUT FLAX DROP COOKIES

MAKES ABOUT 6 DOZEN

Pack these sweet, crisp cookies as a lunchbox treat or serve them as an accompaniment to coffee or tea. Store extras in an airtight container.

1⅓ cups all-purpose flour
1 tsp. baking powder
½ tsp. baking soda
¼ tsp. freshly grated nutmeg
⅛ tsp. salt
⅓ cup milled flaxseed

⅓ cup shortening
⅓ cup butter, softened
1½ cups brown sugar, packed
1 large egg
½ tsp. vanilla extract
⅔ cup chopped toasted walnuts

Heat oven to 350°F. Lightly oil baking sheets or line with parchment paper. In a medium bowl, combine flour, baking powder, baking soda, nutmeg, salt, and flaxseed and stir until mixed. With a mixer, beat shortening, butter and sugar until light and fluffy. Add egg and vanilla and beat well. Gradually add flour mixture to butter mixture, mixing just until combined. Stir in walnuts. Drop cookie dough by heaping teaspoonfuls onto baking sheets about 2 inches apart. Bake for 12 to 15 minutes, until lightly browned and firm to the touch. Cool on a rack.

INDEX